W9-AZD-057

ELEANOR
ROOSEVELT

FIRST LADY OF THE WORLD

SPECIAL LIVES IN HISTORY THAT BECOME

Signature LIVES

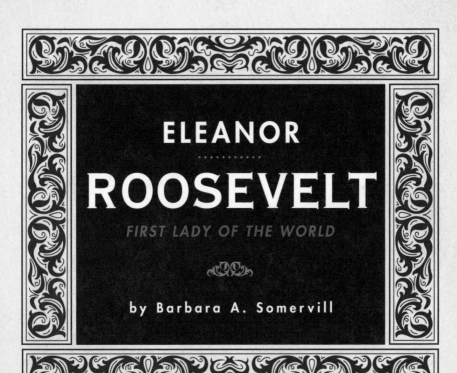

ELEANOR
ROOSEVELT

FIRST LADY OF THE WORLD

by Barbara A. Somervill

Content Adviser: James Wolfinger, Ph.D.,
Assistant Professor, Department of History,
DePaul University

Reading Adviser: Rosemary G. Palmer, Ph.D.,
Department of Literacy, College of Education,
Boise State University

COMPASS POINT BOOKS MINNEAPOLIS, MINNESOTA

Compass Point Books
3109 West 50th Street, #115
Minneapolis, MN 55410

Visit Compass Point Books on the Internet at *www.compasspointbooks.com*
or e-mail your request to *custserv@compasspointbooks.com*

Editor: Jennifer VanVoorst
Lead Designer: Jaime Martens
Photo Researcher: Svetlana Zhurkin
Page Production: Heather Griffin and Bobbie Nuytten
Cartographer: XNR Productions, Inc.
Educational Consultant: Diane Smolinski

Managing Editor: Catherine Neitge
Art Director: Keith Griffin
Editorial Director: Carol Jones
Creative Director: Terri Foley

Library of Congress Cataloging-in-Publication Data
Somervill, Barbara A.
 Eleanor Roosevelt: First Lady of the world / by Barbara A. Somervill.
  p. cm. — (Signature lives)
 Includes bibliographical references and index.
 ISBN-13: 978-0-7565-0992-7 (hardcover)
 ISBN-10: 0-7565-0992-0 (hardcover)
 ISBN-13: 978-0-7565-1856-1 (paperback)
 ISBN-10: 0-7565-1856-3 (paperback)
 1. Roosevelt, Eleanor, 1884–1962—Juvenile literature. 2. Presidents'
spouses—United States—Biography—Juvenile literature. I. Title. II.
Series.
 E807.1.R48S657 2006
 973.917'092—dc22   2005002679

Copyright © 2006 by Compass Point Books
All rights reserved. No part of this book may be reproduced without written permission
from the publisher. The publisher takes no responsibility for the use of any of the
materials or methods described in this book, nor for the products thereof.
Printed in the United States of America.

MODERN AMERICA

Starting in the late 19th century, advancements in all areas of human activity transformed an old world into a new and modern place. Inventions prompted rapid shifts in lifestyle, and scientific discoveries began to alter the way humanity viewed itself. Beginning with World War I, warfare took place on a global scale, and ideas such as nationalism and communism showed that countries were taking a larger view of their place in the world. The combination of all these changes continues to produce what we know as the modern world.

Eleanor Roosevelt

Table of Contents

1 TAKING A STAND

❦❦❦

Eleanor Roosevelt was furious. It was 1939, and Howard University was sponsoring the famous vocalist Marian Anderson in a concert in Washington, D.C.'s Constitution Hall. However, the Daughters of the American Revolution (DAR), the organization that owned the hall and one to which Roosevelt belonged, was refusing to let Anderson sing in its hall. Anderson, an African-American, was one of the finest contraltos in the country, but the DAR had a "No Negroes" policy. Throughout her life, Eleanor Roosevelt had been a woman of principle and of action, and she could not stand for such injustice. She wrote to the leaders of the DAR:

Eleanor Roosevelt presented concert vocalist Marian Anderson with the Spingarn Medal for distinguished achievement by an African-American.

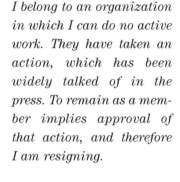

The U.S. secretary of the interior arranged for Marian Anderson's concert to take place instead at the Lincoln Memorial. More than 75,000 people listened as Anderson sang "America," as well as "Gospel Train" and "My Soul Is Anchored in the Lord."

I belong to an organization in which I can do no active work. They have taken an action, which has been widely talked of in the press. To remain as a member implies approval of that action, and therefore I am resigning.

It was just a letter of resignation. But with this letter, written by a first lady to a historic and esteemed organization, civil rights in America had just taken one giant step forward. And, surprisingly, a nationwide poll showed that two-thirds of Americans agreed with Roosevelt.

Eleanor Roosevelt was the first president's wife to have a public life and career of her own. She was a tireless advocate for the poor and the disenfranchised. She would not accept segregation or discrimination. She worked to promote understanding and peace among the world's countries. In a time when women rarely acted so publicly, Roosevelt's words and actions made powerful statements about her vision of society and opened doors for every other woman in the country.

When *Time* magazine looked back over the 20th century, the editors recognized 100 influential

Throughout her career, Roosevelt spoke out on human rights and other issues.

people in politics, science, arts, entertainment, and other fields. Eleanor Roosevelt was the only first lady on the list. Her grace, decency, and quiet dignity moved civil rights, women's rights, and human rights forward a giant step—one public stand at a time. ॐ

2 THE UGLY DUCKLING

❧❧❧

A young girl doesn't look in her mirror and think, "Fifty years from now, I'll be the best-known woman in the world." She doesn't think that a homely face and an awkward body will not matter once she is grown. Little girls have different dreams. They want to be princesses, ballerinas, or singers. They want to be beautiful, loved, and happy. When Eleanor Roosevelt looked in her mirror, all she saw was her family's "ugly duckling." And the feelings attached to that vision of herself were painful.

Eleanor remembered her childhood as cold and lonely. Anna Hall Roosevelt, her beautiful, elegant mother, was a shining light in New York City society. Her charming father, Elliott Roosevelt, was fun-loving and entertaining. The young Roosevelts should

Eleanor Roosevelt remembered her childhood as having been grim and lonely.

have had the happiest of marriages. Unfortunately, Elliott was an alcoholic, and his fondness for drink became the family tragedy.

Elliott and Anna had married in their early 20s. Both came from respectable families. Both had enough money that they could be comfortable and content. Yet, Eleanor later described their marriage: "[My father] married Anna Hall, and tragedy and happiness came walking on each other's heels." What happiness they had was short-lived. Elliott sank deeper into alcoholism, and Anna was powerless to save him.

Anna Eleanor Roosevelt, the couple's first child, arrived a year after they were married. She was born on October 11, 1884. Anna and Elliott called their daughter Eleanor. She was an ugly, wrinkled baby who grew into a quiet, clumsy child. Eleanor loved her parents desperately, but only her father returned that love.

Elliott called his daughter "Little Nell," a name borrowed from Charles Dickens' book, *The Old Curiosity Shop*. Eleanor said, "I never doubted that I stood first in his heart." As a toddler, Eleanor played in the yard of her family's Hempstead, New York, home. Elliott said, "Eleanor is as happy as the day is long, plays with her kitten, the puppy & the little chickens." No one could imagine the heartaches that lay ahead for Eleanor.

By the time Eleanor was 6 years old, Elliott's alcoholism had become a serious problem. He was barely 30 years old, and strong drink was killing him. The Roosevelts headed to France and Italy where Elliott was placed in a hospital that specialized in treating alcoholics.

Eleanor's charming father, Elliott, made Eleanor feel loved and special.

Eleanor found comfort in spending time with her father at their Hempstead, New York, home.

Anna was expecting another child. Her pregnancy and Elliott's illness were all she could handle. She decided to put Eleanor in a Roman Catholic convent school. That way, Eleanor would be cared for, and Anna could deal with the burdens that were already too great for her to handle.

Eleanor felt her parents had deserted her. She wanted attention and reacted as a 6-year-old would. When one of the other girls swallowed a coin, the nuns fussed over her. So, Eleanor decided to try the same tactic. She claimed that she, too, had swallowed a coin. The nuns knew she was lying, though, and called her mother. Anna was filled with shame at her daughter's lie. Later in life, Eleanor admitted:

> *This habit of lying stayed with me for years. My mother did not understand that a child may lie from fear; I myself never understood it until I reached the age when I realized that there was nothing to fear.*

In the next few years, the Roosevelts added two sons to their family: Elliott Junior and Hall. Elliott Senior was in and out of hospitals. That left Anna alone to raise the children.

Eleanor knew that her looks and personality embarrassed and disappointed her gorgeous mother, and she longed to win Anna's affection. Anna, however, seemed unaware that her daughter needed her approval. She called Eleanor "Granny," because Eleanor was so old-fashioned. Anna no doubt thought this a great joke, never realizing how deeply hurt Eleanor was.

Eleanor was 8 years old when her mother caught diphtheria, a

Though she felt alienated from her mother, Eleanor eagerly sought Anna's affection. Anna Roosevelt suffered from terrible headaches, and young Eleanor would often spend hours rubbing her mother's head, trying to make the headaches go away. She later said that the feeling of being useful was the greatest joy she ever experienced.

serious throat infection that can affect the heart and nervous system. The Roosevelt children were shuffled off to Cousin Susie's house. Anna's family sent for Elliott, who was then in a Virginia hospital. He arrived too late: Anna had already died.

Elliott sank under the weight of his grief. Eleanor recalled, "He sat in a big chair. He was dressed all in black, looking very sad. He held out his arms and gathered me to him." Eleanor dreamed that she and her father would now live together with Eleanor running the household. She didn't understand that her father's sickness would not and could not be cured. Her dreams crumbled when her Grandmother Hall took over.

The Roosevelt children moved into Grandmother Hall's home on 37th Street in New York City. It was a large house with a drawing room, dining room, and pantry. There were nine bedrooms, but only two bathrooms.

Grandmother Hall insisted on strict discipline, believing it would build strong character in her grandchildren. She did not believe in spoiling children. She also believed that cold made one healthy and during the winter kept the house so cold that Eleanor had to wear flannel underwear, long black stockings, and heavy flannel petticoats.

Grandmother Hall, uncles Vallie and Eddie, and aunts Pussie and Maude lived there with the three

Roosevelt children. Although the house was always full of people, the adults had little time for the Roosevelt children. A governess named Madeline was responsible for their care, but she was critical and cruel. Eleanor spent much of her time with the cook, butler, housemaids, and laundresses. They were her allies and sided with her when her grandmother punished her. When Grandmother Hall sent

Eleanor also spent time at her grandmother's summer house, Tivoli, where she learned to ride horses.

her to her room without supper, a maid or the butler would sneak a meal up the back stairs.

During their first winter with their grandmother, Eleanor's brothers became sick with scarlet fever, an infection of the skin and throat. Elliot Junior's illness developed into diphtheria, and he died. Eleanor's father fell apart, and on August 14, 1894, 10-year-old Eleanor learned that he had also died. She had suffered three serious losses within just two years.

Eleanor escaped her loneliness in the laundry room. This was hardly the place one would expect to find a future society belle. But Eleanor was desperately lonely, and Mrs. Overhalse, the laundress, provided the company Eleanor needed.

Mrs. Overhalse taught Eleanor how to wash and iron clothes. Laundry was a major affair. There were no automatic washers and dryers in the late 19th century. Hot water boiled in large tin tubs. The clothes were washed by hand and pounded against a metal washboard. Rinsing the clothes, ringing out the extra water, and hanging everything on lines took hours. Then, all the clothing needed ironing. Irons were made of solid metal, and they were placed on stoves to heat.

When Eleanor was 15, Grandmother Hall decided to send her to Allenswood School, near London, England. There, Eleanor studied history and spoke

French with the school's headmistress, a French woman named Marie Souvestre. School life was busy, and rules were strict. The girls were expected to keep their rooms tidy and their beds made. They could take three baths a week—but could only spend 10 minutes at a time in the bathroom. Still, the rules at Allenswood were easier on Eleanor than her grandmother ever was.

Eleanor lived in England for three years while she attended Allenswood School.

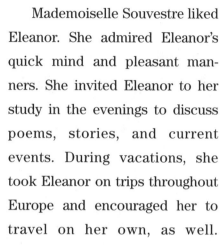

Mademoiselle Souvestre was sympathetic to the poor and downtrodden of society. She taught Eleanor and the other wealthy students at Allenswood that they had a responsibility to help the less-fortunate.

Mademoiselle Souvestre liked Eleanor. She admired Eleanor's quick mind and pleasant manners. She invited Eleanor to her study in the evenings to discuss poems, stories, and current events. During vacations, she took Eleanor on trips throughout Europe and encouraged her to travel on her own, as well. Mademoiselle Souvestre even asked her to plan some of their trips. This was a perfect task for Eleanor. She enjoyed traveling, but she liked the feeling of being useful most of all.

After three years at Allenswood, Eleanor returned to New York City. Once again, she was back in Grandmother Hall's home, living under Grandmother Hall's rules.

Back in New York City, 18-year-old Eleanor stepped into the whirl of high society. She made her debut, a series of events that introduced young women to society and showed they were ready to be married. As a debutante, Eleanor attended parties, dances, concerts, and picnics. She worried, however, that the fashionable, elegant young men she met would ignore her.

Around the time of her debut, Eleanor met her distant cousin Franklin Delano Roosevelt while on a

Franklin Delano Roosevelt was Eleanor's fifth cousin, once removed.

train trip to her grandmother's summer house on the Hudson River. They sat together on the train and talked for hours. Franklin was two years older than Eleanor and a student at Harvard University. Although they had met as children, Eleanor had not seen Franklin for several years. He had developed into a handsome, dashing young gentleman. ᘯ

3 LESSONS LEARNED

Chapter

❧⁓

As a New York City debutante, Eleanor Roosevelt's life mixed dancing and duty. She attended receptions, dinners, balls, and teas, and she became a member of the Junior League, a group that helped support charities with money and volunteer time. Eleanor chose to work with children and women from New York City's East Side slums.

Eleanor had a personal income of about $7,500 a year—a modest fortune in 1903, and she was shocked to meet children whose families survived on just $600 a year. Fathers usually worked 10 hours a day, six days a week for their wages. Eleven dollars a week had to cover housing, clothes, food, and medicine. There was no vacation time, health care, insurance, or other workers' benefits. If a worker

Eleanor's wedding to Franklin Delano Roosevelt was the social event of the season.

was injured on the job, that was simply too bad. Working women and children had it even worse. Many worked 40 or 50 hours a week and earned less than half a man's wages—$5 a week.

Families lived in tenements—huge, shabby apartment buildings. Often, they had no windows, heat, or running water. A family lived in one or two rooms, and a dozen families might share a single bathroom. An extra bedroom was a luxury few could afford.

In the early 20th century, many working families faced cramped and difficult living conditions.

Eleanor worked with people from the Rivington Street Settlement. She taught dancing and calisthenics—a turn-of-the-century version of aerobics. Her classes were designed to help immigrant women and children be healthier. On one occasion, Eleanor investigated a sweatshop on behalf of the Junior League. "I entered my first sweatshop. ... I saw little children of four or five sitting at tables [working] until they dropped with fatigue," she said. Eleanor's sense of common decency made her want to help these people.

In 1903, Eleanor got her first taste of political life. Her uncle James Gracie had died, and another uncle, U.S. President Teddy Roosevelt, came to New York for the funeral. Secret Service agents surrounded the president everywhere he went. Then, Eleanor's Auntie Bye—the president's sister—asked Eleanor to come to Washington, D.C., for a visit. She found herself in a whirl of political and social events. She met diplomats, took tea at the White House with her relatives, and was more than a bit overwhelmed by her experience.

Back in New York, Eleanor was seeing Franklin Roosevelt. Dating is too strong a word for their relationship, because social rules were far too rigid to allow such familiarity. In the early 1900s, society had rules about how young men and women spent time together. Young women never accepted presents from men, except for candy, flowers, or a book. Jewelry was a gift reserved for engaged or married women. There was no kissing until a couple was engaged, and even holding hands was forbidden.

In 1903, Franklin asked Eleanor to marry him. Franklin's mother was not thrilled. Sara Roosevelt thought her son was too young to marry. Besides, she wanted a better-looking wife for her handsome, sociable son. Franklin, however, wanted someone intelligent, witty, and willing to support his political ambitions.

At Sara's insistence, Eleanor and Franklin agreed not to announce their engagement for at least a year. In the meantime, Sara Roosevelt got busy. She was determined to break up the engagement. She even went so far as to take Franklin on a five-week vacation to the Caribbean to try and separate the young couple.

Sara's schemes failed. In 1904, Franklin graduated from Harvard and enrolled in Columbia University's law school. In the fall, Franklin bought Eleanor an engagement ring. Unfortunately, she couldn't wear it because the engagement was still secret. The news of the upcoming marriage was finally released in December. The wedding followed in March 1905.

What a wedding! The ceremony took place on March 17, 1905, in Eleanor's aunt's home in New

York City. Eleanor's Uncle Teddy gave the bride away. Having the president involved definitely made the wedding the social event of the season.

Grandmother Hall dressed all in black velvet as if she were going to a funeral. Franklin's mother wore white trimmed with black lace. The bridesmaids wore taffeta gowns, short veils, and silver-tipped feathers in their hair.

Eleanor's Uncle Teddy Roosevelt was president at the time of her wedding.

The bride and groom exchanged vows and then headed to Franklin's family home in Hyde Park, New York, for a one-week honeymoon. A more exotic honeymoon would follow in the summer when Franklin was on vacation from law school.

The summer honeymoon took Franklin and Eleanor to Europe for three and a half months. Eleanor worried about seasickness, but Franklin wrote, "Eleanor has been a wonderful sailor and hasn't missed a single meal … or lost any either."

The couple toured England and Scotland, France, Germany, Switzerland, and Italy. Eleanor

Eleanor was ferried down the canals of Venice while on her honeymoon.

bought dresses, linens, and fur coats in Paris shops. In Italy, the scanty bathing suits worn by European women shocked Eleanor. Her own bathing kit included a skirt, high-necked blouse, stockings, slippers, sun hat, and gloves. She didn't have to worry about getting a sunburn—not enough skin showed to burn.

Franklin and Eleanor finally headed home, and Sara arranged a rental house for them just three blocks from her own home. The house, at 125 E. 36th Street in New York City, was small and simple. Eleanor asked that a telephone be installed but told her mother-in-law not to worry about having the house wired with electricity. In 1905, few homes had electricity, and many people thought it was dreadfully unsafe. They preferred gaslights that had to be lit each night.

The next few years were typical for a newly married couple of the time. Franklin went off to law school and, later, to work. Eleanor raised their children. Their first child, Anna, was born on May 2, 1906. Eleanor said that from the start Anna etched a permanent place in her heart.

A little more than a year later, a second child arrived. The boy, named James, was born two days before Christmas 1907. The winter was cold and dreary. James seemed plagued by sickness and caught pneumonia. Eleanor was exhausted and slow to recover from childbirth.

Sara Roosevelt decided Franklin and his family needed a home of their own. She bought, decorated, and furnished a new home on 65th Street. Then she

Franklin's mother, Sara, dominated the early days of his marriage. She often paid for additional expenses, and even went so far as to make Eleanor give up her work in the slums. Because Franklin did not earn much money, Sara offered his family an allowance so that they could live more comfortably.

moved herself—to a house she had built right next door. Eleanor's new house did not suit her taste at all, and she resented her mother-in-law's interference. Franklin saw no problems in the arrangement, however. Franklin and Sara won that battle, and Eleanor settled into the house against her wishes.

Franklin's and Eleanor's personalities were opposites. Franklin was a sociable man, a joiner, and an athlete. He belonged to the Knickerbocker Club and the Harvard Club. Franklin loved dancing, entertaining, and going to parties. He played golf and tennis, and sailed in the summer. Winters found him skating on the Hudson River, tobaggoning, and hunting.

Eleanor, on the other hand, was no athlete. She was afraid of water, never sailed, and her only sport was horseback riding. She was self-conscious and awkward at parties and shunned life in the public eye. She spent her time supporting her charities and working for causes she believed in. Still, they got along well enough, with Franklin calling his wife "Babs" and the children "chicks." Eleanor later wrote, "Success in marriage depends on being able when you get over being in love, to really love. … You never know anyone until you marry them."

March 1909 brought the birth of Franklin D. Roosevelt Jr. While this baby was the largest of the Roosevelts' children, he was not healthy. During the

In 1908, Eleanor and Franklin posed for a formal portrait with children Anna (right) and James.

summer, young Franklin seemed to have trouble breathing. By the fall, the trouble became serious. The doctor said Franklin Junior suffered from heart trouble. On November 1, 1909, 7-month-old Franklin Junior died. Grief flattened Eleanor like a bulldozer. ✎

4 THE SENATOR'S WIFE, THE GOVERNOR'S WIFE

Chapter

❧⟨∽⟩❧

It was 1910. Franklin Delano Roosevelt decided it was time to begin fulfilling his political ambitions. New York's Dutchess County Democrats needed a candidate for the state senate, but the election would be an uphill battle for them. The county's voters usually voted Republican. Still, Franklin Roosevelt was young, friendly, and popular. He had a slim chance.

Eleanor said:

> *I listened to all his plans with a great deal of interest. ... It never occurred to me that I had any part. I felt I must [agree] in whatever he might decide and be willing to go to Albany.*

Franklin Roosevelt began his political career as a state senator in New York.

Eleanor Roosevelt traveled with her husband as he met voters in Dutchess County, New York.

At the time, she was probably right. In 1910, most people believed that a woman's place was in the home. Women did not enter politics. They couldn't even vote, although the fight for women's suffrage—or right to vote—was pushing forward.

Eleanor gave birth to another son later that year. The Roosevelts named him Elliott, after Eleanor's father. Franklin's campaign rolled on, and everyone was shocked when he won. He and Eleanor moved to Albany, New York, where Franklin took his seat in the state senate. Eleanor was pleased to be away from her mother-in-law. She was finally able to run her household the way she chose.

In 1912, Franklin was up for reelection. He was

sick at the time and wasn't able to campaign, so Eleanor took over. She turned out to be a surprisingly good campaigner. Franklin won by 1,500 votes—a healthy margin for a county election. Democrat Woodrow Wilson won the presidential election that year.

Always ambitious, Franklin was looking to further his political career. In 1913, he left Albany to become assistant secretary of the Navy under President Wilson. The large Roosevelt family seemed to invade Washington, D.C., with their many children, servants, and trunks filled with clothes, toys, books, and household goods.

Eleanor was becoming accustomed to the role of political wife and spent her days fulfilling the social obligations that came with her husband's job. She wrote:

> *Nearly all the women at that time were the slaves of the Washington social system. … I was perfectly certain that I had nothing to offer of an individual nature and that my only chance of doing my duty as the wife of a public official was to do exactly as the majority of the other women were doing.*

Eleanor credited much of her political education to Franklin's political adviser, Louis Howe. He informed her of the issues surrounding her husband's various campaigns and positions, coached her on making speeches and appearing in public, and encouraged her in her literary work. Eleanor named Howe as one of the most important people in her life.

In the next few years, the Roosevelt family welcomed two more sons. In 1914, Eleanor gave birth to the second Franklin Junior, and in 1916, another son, named John, was born.

Raising the children became a constant battle of wills between Eleanor, Franklin, and Franklin's mother, Sara. Eleanor most often lost the fight. Franklin spoiled his children. He allowed them to run wild and found them great fun. Sara, though iron-willed, was an indulgent grandmother. She had tried to break off her son's engagement, interfered in his marriage, and now she wanted to raise Franklin's children "her way." She spoiled the children, who quickly learned that if their mother said "no," they could go to Grandma and get their way. Eleanor recalled, "Franklin's children were more my mother-in-law's children than mine."

Franklin's responsibilities with the Navy expanded as Europe entered into World War I in 1914. President Wilson had hoped to keep America out of the war. Despite his efforts, Americans began losing their lives as German submarines sank ocean liners—regardless of who was on the passenger list. On February 3, 1917, the USS *Housatonic* sank after being struck by a German torpedo. Though President Wilson did not want to go to war, Germany's aggressive actions forced him to make a decision. The United States declared war against

Germany and its allies on April 6, 1917.

Franklin worked long hours at the Navy. Eleanor, too, wanted to help the war effort. She volunteered at the Red Cross canteen two or three times a week. She helped organize the Navy branch of the Red Cross. That group distributed wool for volunteers to knit. Socks were the main product and were shipped abroad to the military, along with chocolate, cigarettes, magazines, and other goods.

Canteen work was a definite change for Eleanor. At home, she had servants to cook, clean house, and help with the children. At the canteen, she pitched in

Franklin, with his sons Elliott and James, enjoyed spending time with Sara Roosevelt at their summer home off the coast of Maine.

President Woodrow Wilson appeared before the U.S. Congress to announce the start of the war.

with whatever work was needed. She made and served coffee, talked with servicemen, and even mopped the floors.

At least once a week, Eleanor visited the local Navy hospital. She brought flowers, cigarettes, and chocolate to the patients. Mostly, though, she just sat and talked with injured men who were lonely and missing their wives and families.

In addition to the war, Eleanor had difficult personal issues to deal with. In 1918, she was shocked to discover love letters to her husband from Lucy Mercer, a woman who for the past several years had worked as Eleanor's personal secretary. Eleanor was devastated. She offered Franklin a divorce. Franklin's political adviser, Louis Howe, as well as his mother, advised him that a divorce would mean the end of his political career. The couple decided to stay together, but the experience changed Eleanor forever. It became one of the great turning points in her life. She said, "The bottom dropped out of my ... world, and I faced myself ... honestly for the first time." She resolved to become more self-reliant and began to more actively pursue her own interests.

When the war ended and Eleanor was no longer needed in the Red Cross canteen, she took up the concerns of working women. She met representatives from 19 countries at a meeting of the International Congress for Women Workers. This group promoted equal pay for women doing the same work as men. It also promoted better working conditions and opposed child labor. After Eleanor's experience with New York City's East Side slum dwellers, she was happy to work with a group that could make changes for poor women and children.

In August 1920, the 19th Amendment to the Constitution was ratified, finally giving women the right to vote. Eleanor joined the League of Women Voters, an organization that helped educate women about politics and voting. And in November, she and millions of other American women cast their votes for U.S. president.

That year, Franklin was a Democratic candidate for vice president, along with Democratic presidential candidate James Cox. Roosevelt and Cox campaigned across the country by train. Their "whistle-stop" campaign often found them pulling into a train station, speaking from a platform at the back of the caboose, and pulling out within an hour. In the end, the voters wanted a change from the Woodrow Wilson era, and the Democrats lost to Republican Warren Harding and his running mate Calvin Coolidge.

The year 1921 was a turning point in the Roosevelts' lives. The family was enjoying the summer at their retreat at Campobello Island in New Brunswick, Canada. Franklin brought friends along for sailing and deep-sea fishing. He felt chilled and soon became seriously ill. Franklin had fallen victim to infantile paralysis, a disease also known as polio.

The family quickly returned to New York, with Franklin traveling on a stretcher. Little was known

Polio is a serious infection caused by a virus. It attacks the nerve cells that control the muscles in many parts of the body. In the past, epidemics of polio were common and were greatly feared because the disease left many patients paralyzed for life. In 1955, however, a vaccine against the disease was introduced. Since then, polio has been nearly eliminated in developed countries.

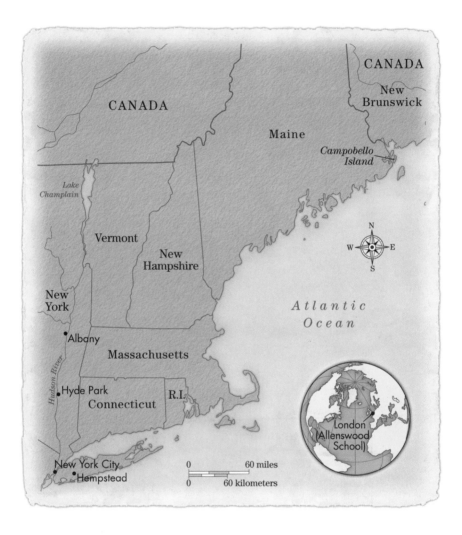

Eleanor lived most of her life on the East Coast.

about polio at the time. There was no vaccine to prevent this dreadful disease, as there is today. The only thing that could be done was a painful procedure of putting the victim's legs in plaster casts to stretch the muscles.

Sara Roosevelt told her son that he should retire

In 1925, Eleanor Roosevelt built a small cottage near Val-Kill Stream in Hyde Park, New York. She later said that she felt this cottage was her first real home. In 1927, Eleanor and two friends started a furniture factory there. Val-Kill Industries, as the business was called, employed farmers and young people from the Hyde Park area.

from politics, but Eleanor disagreed. So did Dr. Draper, the family doctor. He recommended a return to as normal and active a life as possible. Franklin went to work at the Fidelity and Deposit Company's New York City branch, but he continued therapy to regain the use of his legs. Within a year, he could walk with crutches.

Meanwhile, Eleanor continued to pursue her interest in women's rights and worked to raise money for the women's division of the Democratic State Committee. She worked actively for the Women's Trade Union League in support of working women. She also wrote antiwar articles for the *Women's Democratic News* and taught American literature, English, and American history at the Todhunter School, near the family's home in Hyde Park, New York.

By 1928, Franklin could walk with a cane, although he usually got around in a wheelchair. New York's Democratic governor, Alfred Smith, wanted to run for U.S. president, so the state needed a new governor. Despite his physical challenges, Franklin Roosevelt ran for governor and

In 1929, Franklin Roosevelt was sworn in as governor of New York.

won by a very narrow margin.

As New York's governor, Roosevelt could have had an easy term, except for one problem: The New York stock market crashed in October 1929, and the United States sank into an economic slump that would last for 10 years. Even Governor Roosevelt couldn't defeat the financial disaster that strangled the country. ✑

Chapter
5 THE GREAT DEPRESSION AND A NEW DEAL

⥷∽⥸

October 29, 1929—the day the stock market crashed—became known as Black Tuesday. The crash occurred because too many people bought stocks on credit. Stockbrokers loaned clients money to buy stock, using other stock the clients already owned to secure the loans. When stock values dropped, people in debt could not pay what they owed. This started an economic cycle of losses that sent the nation into what became known as the Great Depression.

The Great Depression was a worldwide disaster. Few countries were spared. As bad as things were in the United States, they were worse in Europe, where a wheelbarrow filled with money could barely buy a loaf of bread.

The 1929 stock market crash left many Americans unemployed.

People, companies, and banks had borrowed against their stocks and owed huge sums of money. For individuals, the crash meant losing income—and more. Debts grew too great to pay off. Millions of people lost their farms and homes; many lived in shacks or became homeless. Men, women, and children stood in lines at soup kitchens to have one meal a day.

Many companies had invested their profits in stocks in order to earn more money. When the stock market crashed, companies lost money needed to build new factories or support their employees. Within a short time, companies began closing factories, and workers lost their jobs. As unemployment grew, people had no money to buy new products. Business income dropped to nothing, so more factories closed.

Banks also had investments that suffered from the crash. Banks put money into stocks and loaned money to individuals and businesses. When stock values collapsed, neither people nor companies could pay back their loans. Customers tried to get money out of their bank accounts, but the banks had spent more money than they had. They couldn't give people their money. Banks closed, and customers—even ones who hadn't invested in stocks—lost their savings.

For three years, the Great Depression grew

Agricultural workers in the West were hit hard by the Great Depression.

worse. President Herbert Hoover had developed an economic recovery plan, but it simply didn't work. In New York, Governor Franklin Roosevelt decided to take political action. He saw a country in which the gap between rich and poor was too great. One in four workers had no work. Children were starving.

Franklin decided to run for president on the Democratic Party ticket. He developed a plan to rebuild the economy that he called the "New Deal." Voters were fed up, and in 1932, they chose the New Deal over the ineffective Hoover.

Eleanor was not pleased with Franklin's victory. She said, "I never wanted to be a President's wife, and don't want it now. For him, of course, I'm glad— sincerely." But for Eleanor, the presidency meant living in the White House, representing the country, and completely losing her privacy. She compared being first lady to living in a goldfish bowl. She was the goldfish, and the entire world peeked in on her. Eleanor had seen firsthand what it meant to be the first lady; her aunt Edith had played that role for seven and a half years, as wife of President Teddy Roosevelt. Eleanor was afraid she would have to give up working on the projects that meant so much to her.

As first lady, Eleanor had a number of social and ceremonial duties to perform. She chose menus and made seating charts for official dinners. She also socialized with citizens and politicians at official receptions and answered letters from around the world. Still, she found time to involve herself in the president's new economic programs.

Even as first lady, Eleanor preferred to drive herself to public appearances. The president and his adviser insisted that she have a bodyguard and hired Earl Miller, a New York state trooper, to travel with her. Over time, Miller became one of Eleanor's closest friends.

In the first 100 days of his presidency, Franklin Roosevelt started work on his New Deal. People called the New Deal

"alphabet soup" government. Every program had a name, and every name was referred to by letters. There was the EBA (Emergency Banking Act), the

The Roosevelts (with son James, at right) moved into the White House in 1933.

CCC (Civilian Conservation Corps), the WPA (Works Progress Administration), the NYA (National Youth Administration), and so on.

The president's programs provided relief for the poor and homeless, created jobs, and encouraged the economy to kick-start itself again. The federal government managed the programs and paid for them with government money. And the programs worked. Millions of out-of-work people found themselves working—and earning—again, and in doing so, paying the taxes needed to fund more programs.

The Civilian Conservation Corps (CCC), for example, put 2.5 million unmarried men to work. The pay was $30 per month, plus food and housing in a tent. Over eight years, the CCC planted more than 200 million trees in national parks and campgrounds. The men built roads, cleaned up beaches, and stocked rivers and lakes with fish. Eleanor Roosevelt visited many of the camps and applauded the work done by the CCC. She said:

> *I feel the work of the CCC camps has enriched many communities. Aside from the fact that it has taken boys who might have drifted into evil ways and kept them busy, it has given them better health and skill with which to face the world.*

Although programs such as the CCC pleased

Eleanor, they were not enough. She wanted more. She wanted to shake up society, providing better housing, health care, and education for all citizens— not just white men. Her two favorite New Deal projects were Arthurdale and the NYA. Arthurdale was an experimental community built in West Virginia. The project was developed under the Subsistence Homestead Act (SHA). Basically, the government bought a farm and built 200 houses on the land. The homes were small, but had electricity, indoor bathrooms, and refrigerators—the last two items at Eleanor's insistence.

CCC workers relocated beavers in Idaho's Salmon National Forest.

Children at Arthurdale played outside in their yard.

Eleanor described Arthurdale:

> *The chicken farm ... is doing very well.
> The entire output of eggs is being sold to
> the state [hospital] at Hopemont. ... The
> homesteaders have done well with their
> pigs and the dairy co-operative is about
> to start. They are planning to specialize
> in Jersey cows producing cream which
> will be saleable in Washington [D.C.]. ...
> The last forty houses ... are delightfully
> planned and so livable that I would like
> to have one. Such houses as I had an
> opportunity to stop in today looked com-
> fortable and homelike.*

The National Youth Administration (NYA) put teenagers to work. Teens received training and help finding part-time jobs. This was very important. Many teenagers lived in homes where there was too little money to cover food or clothing. Their pay bought milk, eggs, bread, and fruit. Eleanor praised the NYA, saying, "It was one of the occasions on which I was proud that the right thing was done regardless of political considerations."

Eleanor's good friend Mary McLeod Bethune ran the African-American branch of the NYA. Eleanor hated discrimination of any kind, but she especially resented discrimination against women, Native Americans, and African-Americans. Still, segregation was the rule in the 1930s, whether Eleanor liked it or not. A separate branch of the NYA helped African-American teens, particularly those in inner cities. Bethune's efforts helped thousands of inner city black teens get jobs and support their families. Eleanor wrote of her friend, "One could not meet her and not

Mary McLeod Bethune (1875–1955) worked to improve educational opportunities for African-Americans. In 1904, she opened a school for African-American girls in Daytona Beach, Florida. The school became a coeducational college in 1923 and is now called Bethune-Cookman College. As director of the Division of Negro Affairs of the National Youth Administration (NYA), Bethune was the first African-American woman to head a federal agency.

In 1960, Eleanor Roosevelt was presented with the McLeod Bethune Human Right Award.

recognize her sincerity … She is the kindest, gentlest person I have ever met."

Eleanor continued to work for causes that interested her, even when they fell outside the realm of her husband's programs. For example, she was the first U.S. first lady to hold regular press conferences, to which only female reporters were invited. This move forced newspapers to hire more female reporters in order to ensure access to the first lady.

She also discussed issues such as the pay and working conditions of women employed in sweatshops. And she continued to be interested in the country's young people. She wanted to stop child labor, because she'd seen 5- and 6-year-old children working 50 and 60 hours a week for less than half what men earned. She also wanted to make sure children were being educated and fed. She learned that in New York City many teachers were feeding hungry students with their own money. Eleanor said, "I think we should all give them thanks, and make sure that no child suffers from malnutrition."

Eleanor Roosevelt held her women-only press conferences at the suggestion of her friend Lorena Hickok, a leading political reporter whom Roosevelt had met when Hickok was assigned to cover Franklin's 1932 campaign. "Hick" gave up her assignment in 1933, when her growing friendship with Eleanor prevented her from being objective in covering the Roosevelts. Roosevelt and Hick continued to be close friends for the rest of their lives.

Eleanor even served a "7¢ lunch" at the White House. The menu included stuffed eggs, mashed potatoes, prune pudding, bread, and coffee. Eleanor made her point: People could eat wholesome food for very little money. Few first ladies would have had the nerve to serve such a meal. But then, Eleanor Roosevelt wasn't the typical first lady.

6 THE FIRST LADY

Chapter

᭡᭡᭡

Eleanor Roosevelt provided newspaper reporters with plenty of material for their articles. She was the first president's wife to travel by plane, go down into a mine, travel without her husband, ride on a cable car, or earn money.

Many people criticized Roosevelt for her independence. Others resented her power over the president. Some recalled seeing her sit across from Franklin, hold his hands in hers, and talk him into her point of view. That she was proven right on many occasions did not stop the critics. They called her "Empress Eleanor" and "Madam President." Roosevelt later wrote:

In 1939, Eleanor Roosevelt entertained England's queen at the White House.

*In the last analysis you have to be friends
with yourself twenty-four hours of the day.
If you run counter to others now and then,
you have enemies, but life would become
unbearable if you thought about it all of the
time, so you have to ignore the critics. ...
If you are honest, you will always be your
own most severe critic.*

*Eleanor
enjoyed air
travel, even in
its early days,
and she trav-
eled frequently
by plane.*

In 1936, Roosevelt started writing a daily newspaper column called "My Day." At first, the column
appeared in only 20 newspapers nationwide. By the
end of the year, however, 60 papers carried "My
Day." The topics she wrote about covered every-

thing from parenting to politics. The column ran six days a week, from 1936 until her death in 1962, and she rarely missed a deadline.

In 1936, African-American singer Marian Anderson entertained Eleanor and Franklin Roosevelt at the White House. Ms. Anderson was one of the first African-Americans to do so. Mrs. Roosevelt wrote in "My Day":

Eleanor Roosevelt was unique as a first lady in that she earned an income for her "My Day" column, as well as for lectures and radio broadcasts. But even her harshest critics could not say much about the money. After all, Roosevelt gave her earnings to charity.

My husband and I had a rare treat Wednesday night in listening to Marian Anderson, a [black] contralto, who had made a great success in Europe and this country. She sang three Schubert songs and finished with two Negro spirituals.

Inviting Marian Anderson to perform at the White House made a major statement to 1930s society. Roosevelt's resignation from the Daughters of the American Revolution three years later over their refusal to let Anderson sing at Constitution Hall made an even more dramatic statement—one that gave a tremendous boost to the growing civil rights movement.

With each passing year, the first lady traveled farther, shook more hands, and entertained more people. In 1937, Roosevelt traveled more than 43,000 miles (68,800 kilometers). She gave 100 speeches and poured countless cups of tea. She was a social reformer, but she never forgot to be a mother, a wife, a hostess, or a friend. Despite her political critics, ordinary people loved Eleanor. A poll showed that she was more popular than the president. More than 67 percent of Americans approved of Eleanor, while only 58 percent approved of Franklin.

All this popularity didn't inflate Eleanor's ego. In 1939, the Roosevelts hosted a visit by England's King George VI and Queen Elizabeth, the parents of England's present-day Queen Elizabeth II. The king and queen visited them in Hyde Park, and Eleanor planned a typical American picnic, with hot dogs and baked beans. Again, her plans met with criticism. Eleanor told people, including her mother-in-law, not to worry; there would be plenty of food, she assured them. She would also serve other American favorites, including smoked turkey, cured ham, and strawberry shortcake.

In the fall of 1939, Europe was moving toward a second world war. The United States didn't want to get involved. Eleanor, mother of four sons, wanted peace. She urged, "Let's ask our leaders not to weaken their stand against war, but to tell us what more could be done for permanent peace."

At the same time, a change was underway in the

U.S. military. Historically, troops were segregated by race. Many white soldiers and sailors did not trust African-Americans in the military. In the early 1940s, young black pilots trained in Tuskegee, Alabama. They were called the Tuskegee Airmen. On one of her many tours, Eleanor Roosevelt visited the 332nd Fighter Group in Tuskegee. Charles Anderson, the flight instructor, offered to take her for a ride. The Secret Service agents protecting Eleanor didn't know what to do. They called President Roosevelt

Many of the Tuskegee Airmen became decorated war heroes in World War II.

and asked his advice. He said, "Well, if she wants to do it, there's nothing we can do to stop her." Photographs of Eleanor with the pilot appeared in just about every newspaper in the country. Her support of the Tuskegee Airmen became part of the Eleanor Roosevelt legend.

In 1940, Franklin Roosevelt ran for his third term as president of the United States. No previous president had served more than two terms, but this fact was not what threatened his candidacy. Many were reluctant to support Roosevelt because they disapproved of Henry A. Wallace, his controversial choice for vice president. Eleanor spoke at the Democratic Party's national convention and encouraged the delegates to support Wallace. No first lady had ever spoken at such an event. In the end, the delegates supported Wallace, and in November 1940, the country showed their support for President Roosevelt by electing him to his third term by an overwhelming margin.

Meanwhile, the war raged on in Europe and the Pacific. Eleanor urged the government to allow more European refugees to enter the United States, but the government was trying to minimize U.S. involvement in the conflict. The United States sold food, cloth, weapons, and other goods to England and its allies. The plan was to provide goods but to stay out of the war. That changed on December 7,

1941. The Japanese bombed Pearl Harbor, Hawaii, a United States naval base. Franklin Roosevelt delivered a speech, broadcast by radio across the country, in which he called December 7th "a date that will live in infamy." The United States was at war. ॐ

The USS Arizona *(at right) sank during the Japanese surprise attack on Pearl Harbor.*

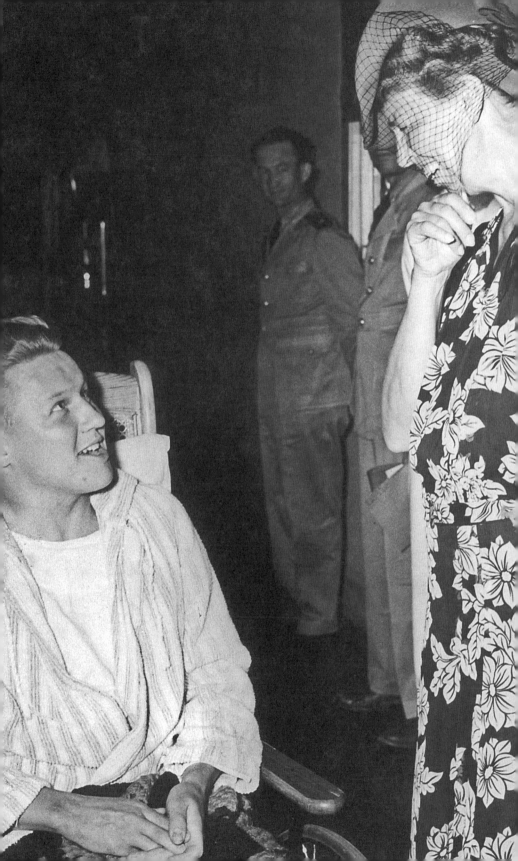

Chapter

7 WORLD WAR II

❦

All White House activity was now focused on supporting a war that stretched across oceans and continents. Like many Americans, Roosevelt bought war bonds that helped pay the massive costs of a worldwide war. She answered letters from soldiers and sailors and wrote to their families. She visited military hospitals throughout the United States and wherever else in the world she visited. She never passed by a bed without talking to the patient lying in it. She'd lean over, hold the patient's hand, and smile. She listened to them and encouraged them. This practice added up to thousands upon thousands of private chats.

The Roosevelts' four sons joined the military along with millions of other men. Eleanor wrote:

Eleanor Roosevelt visited a wounded soldier at a naval hospital during World War II.

I imagine every mother felt as I did when I said good-by to the children during the war. I had a feeling that I might be saying good-bye for the last time. It was a sort of precursor of what it would be like if your children were killed. Life had to go on and you had to do what was required of you, but something inside of you quietly died.

She worried about her sons, but she never forgot the women and children struggling at home.

While soldiers fought in Europe and the Pacific, people back in the United States did their part to help the war effort. Rationing began, covering sugar, coffee, meat, butter, and canned goods. Every citizen had a ration book, and each week, people could only buy as much sugar, for example, as they had sugar ration stamps. Besides food, rubber, tires, gasoline, and shoes were rationed as well. People began carpooling or walking to work. Even the first lady did her part. In a letter to a serviceman, Roosevelt wrote:

Eleanor Roosevelt believed that continuing to promote democracy in the United States was an important part of the war effort. She believed that though the country had won World War I, it had lost the peace. In a speech broadcast on the radio, she encouraged Americans to take strength from one another and dedicate themselves to preserving democracy at home.

Like everyone else, we are trying to conserve gas and tires. I have a bicycle which one of

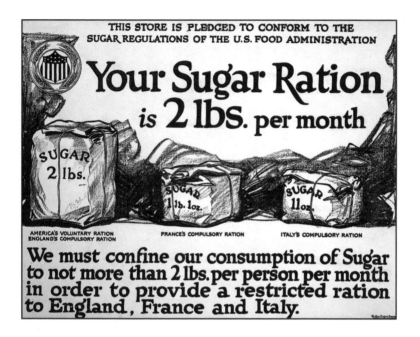

THIS STORE IS PLEDGED TO CONFORM TO THE
SUGAR REGULATIONS OF THE U.S. FOOD ADMINISTRATION

Your Sugar Ration
is 2 lbs. per month

SUGAR
2 lbs.

SUGAR
1 lb. 1oz.

SUGAR
11oz.

AMERICA'S VOLUNTARY RATION
ENGLAND'S COMPULSORY RATION   FRANCE'S COMPULSORY RATION   ITALY'S COMPULSORY RATION

**We must confine our consumption of Sugar
to not more than 2 lbs. per person per month
in order to provide a restricted ration
to England, France and Italy.**

*my boys gave me several years ago, and I
have taken to bicycle-riding again. ... I find
it very convenient ... for running errands
in the neighborhood.*

A war-era poster compared U.S. ration sizes to those of England, France, and Italy.

The growing war effort finally brought the Great Depression to a halt. Factories opened and people worked long hours. The war required processed food, clothing, blankets, boots, weapons, ammunition, vehicles, medicine—hundreds of items made in factories. As men enlisted in the military, women went to work in factories. Roosevelt worried about who was taking care of the nation's children while their mothers turned out planes, tanks, and tents.

In Portland, Oregon, Roosevelt visited the Kaiser

During World War II, women who worked in the war industries were referred to by the name "Rosie the Riveter."

shipyards. With her ever-present smile and engaging manner, she talked the Kaiser management into providing on-site day care for working mothers. The center became a model day-care facility where children of different ages and races played together. It was another Roosevelt "first."

Roosevelt's war efforts spread beyond U.S. borders. Late in 1942, she went to London to visit King George and Queen Elizabeth. The trip was kept secret right up until she left. There were worries about the Germans shooting down the first lady's plane. Roosevelt had gone to school near London and was familiar with all the sights. Still, she was shocked by the destruction she saw. The German blitz had bombed churches, schools, homes, factories, and even Buckingham Palace.

The king and queen apologized for the state of Roosevelt's room when she stayed with them at the palace. Like the rest of London, the royals followed strict blackout rules. Broken palace windows had been covered with plywood. Heavy curtains kept light from seeping through the few remaining glass windows. Fuel conservation was a must, and Roosevelt found only a small fire warming her apartments. She wrote:

Their Majesties took me to visit St. Paul's Cathedral. It was my first view of the destruction which has leveled whole blocks of houses. It is remarkable that St. Paul's still stands, in spite of considerable damage. Its firefighters spent night after night sleeping in the crypt, ready to spring to their post should they be needed.

But even more poignant is the destruction that we viewed a little bit later in Stepney. Here the crowded population lived over small shops and in rows of two-story houses. Today there is only one-third of the population left, and each empty building speaks of a personal tragedy.

> *During the war, Roosevelt carried a prayer in her pocket to remind her that someone somewhere died for her that day and to encourage her to ask and answer the question, "Am I worth dying for?"*

While in London, Roosevelt visited Red Cross clubs and talked with servicemen and women from many countries. She took names and home addresses of the Americans she met. Once back in the United States, Roosevelt wrote to their parents and told them that she'd seen their sons and daughters.

On one visit, Roosevelt learned that many soldiers suffered from blisters because they did not have wool socks. She couldn't do much about ending the war, but sore feet were an easy fix for Roosevelt. She wrote a letter of complaint to General Dwight D. Eisenhower, who looked into the problem and responded:

> *I find that we have not only made all normal issues, but we have at the minute two and one-half million pairs of light woolen sox in warehouses. ... I have already started the various commanders on a check-up to see that no man needs to march without proper footgear.*

Roosevelt's European visit was a hit. Everywhere she went, she made a lasting impression. When the troops lined up to greet her in the rain, she walked along the line and spoke to each person. If they got wet, so did Roosevelt. After she left England, Prime Minister Winston Churchill wrote to Roosevelt, "You certainly have left golden footprints behind you."

Prime Minister Winston Churchill gave the "V for victory" sign.

The year 1943 took Eleanor Roosevelt in the opposite direction from England—to the Pacific war zone. She would write newspaper and magazine articles as she traveled, so she needed to bring her typewriter with her. The first lady had a 44-pound (19.8-kilogram) baggage limit, including the typewriter. Luckily, she could wear a Red Cross uniform, which saved on bringing many clothes. Roosevelt donated her earnings from articles written on the trip to the Red Cross and the American Friends Service Committee.

Roosevelt arrived on Christmas Island, near Indonesia—her first time visiting the Tropics. She said, "When I walked into the room after supper and, putting on the light, found my floor completely covered with little red bugs, I nearly disgraced myself by screaming." Instead, she stamped out as many of the bugs as she could.

On this trip, Roosevelt visited hospitals, rest homes, camps, and recreation centers. As in England, she took down names and home addresses of the Americans she met. Letters to families would follow. No island was too small, no outpost too remote for a visit from Roosevelt. She slept on hard cots and lumpy mattresses. She ate whatever food was served without making a fuss or demanding special privileges. And she walked miles and miles and miles—all with a smile on her face.

Before the trip, Admiral William Halsey had been against Roosevelt's arrival. He worried about keeping her safe. He had a war to win in the Pacific, and baby-sitting Eleanor Roosevelt wasn't a high priority. By the time she left, however, Halsey had become her biggest fan. He said:

Roosevelt visited sailors at Pearl Harbor in 1943.

> *Here is what she did in twelve hours: she inspected two Navy hospitals, took a boat*

*to an officer's rest home and had lunch
there, returned and inspected an Army
hospital, reviewed the 2nd Marine
Raider Battalion, made a speech at a
service club, attended a reception, and
was guest of honor at a dinner.*

*She went into every ward, stopped at
every bed, and spoke to every patient. ...
She walked for miles, and she saw
patients who were grievously and grue-
somely wounded. But I marveled most at
their expressions as she leaned over
them. It was a sight I will never forget.*

Back home, Roosevelt met the usual demands of
being first lady: answering more than 100,000 letters
a year, traveling thousands of miles, being the White
House hostess, and attending dinners and charity
functions. Still, there was no aspect of the war effort
too small for her attention. When the government
needed used cooking fat to make smokeless gun-
powder and medicines, Roosevelt urged housewives
to save bacon grease, cooking lard, any used fats
they had. As with all her other ventures, the fat-col-
lection plea was answered by many.

On April 12, 1945, Eleanor gave a speech at a
charity event in Washington, D.C. Franklin, now in
his fourth term as president, was at Warm Springs,
Georgia, having therapy for his paralysis. It was in
many ways a typical day—until a messenger came to

Eleanor's event and asked her to return to the White House. She later said, "I did not even ask why. I knew down in my heart that something dreadful had happened." Franklin Roosevelt had died of a brain hemorrhage.

Roosevelt cabled her soldier sons immediately. The war was nearly over in Germany but continued to be fought in the Pacific. Her sons were all still in uniform and on active duty. The telegram read, "Father slept away. He would expect you to carry on and finish your jobs."

Roosevelt attended a dinner put on by the Daughters of the Depression in 1945.

Roosevelt changed into a black dress and called Vice President Harry Truman to the Oval Office. She told Truman that the president had died. Truman was shocked. He asked, "Is there anything I can do for you?" Roosevelt replied, "Is there anything we can do for you? For you are the one in trouble now."

The next day, Eleanor traveled on the funeral train back to Hyde Park. Franklin had asked to be

Many public figures gathered in Hyde Park to attend Franklin Roosevelt's funeral.

buried in the rose garden of his family home. She watched out the window as the train slipped northward through the darkness. At each station, each crossroads, people stood at attention. They paid their final respects to a man who had seen them through the worst economic depression and the worst war on record. Throughout the funeral and the days afterward, Roosevelt carried herself with the dignity and gentleness she'd shown throughout her marriage.

After she left the White House, Roosevelt realized how much had changed for her. She wrote, "One cannot say good-by to people with whom one has lived and who have served one well without deep emotion, but at last even that was over. I was on my own." ✒

Chapter

8 ON HER OWN

‹∽∾∽›

Eleanor Roosevelt's first business after dealing with her husband's death was to figure out how she would be able to live. She often remarked that she left the White House poorer than when she arrived. In 1946, her income amounted to $80,000 from various sources. Unfortunately, taxes amounted to $54,000. That left her only $26,000.

How could she live on that amount of money? She still earned money for her "My Day" column. She was also paid for radio and television appearances, and her book *This I Remember* sold well. President Harry Truman appointed Roosevelt to the American delegation to the United Nations. At the time, the United Nations was a new concept. Roosevelt earned $12,000 as a U.N. delegate.

As a delegate to the United Nations, Eleanor Roosevelt was able to discuss her views with representatives from many countries.

Roosevelt believed in both the idea and the ideal of the United Nations. The end of World War II and the development of the atomic bomb made lasting peace a priority. She said:

> *I think that if the atomic bomb did nothing more, it scared the people to the point where they realized that either they must do something about preventing war or there is a chance that there might be a morning when we would not wake up.*

The first formal meetings of the United Nations took place in London in 1946. Roosevelt and the rest of the American delegation boarded the *Queen Elizabeth* in New York and headed to London.

Few delegates worked as hard as Eleanor Roosevelt. She read all the briefing material the State Department provided. She attended all the meetings and press conferences. She got up early each morning, walked several miles to keep in shape, and headed back to work for the rest of the day.

At the first official U.N. meeting, Roosevelt made a slight error. Her assigned seat was at the end of the American delegation, right next to the representatives from the Soviet Union. By mistake, she took V.V. Kuznetzov's seat. Kuznetzov had a sense of humor and offered to let Roosevelt join the Soviet delegation since she was sitting in their space. Although she politely declined, both groups had a good laugh.

The first order of business at the meeting was to choose a president for the U.N. General Assembly. The delegates chose Paul Henri Spaak from Belgium. Spaak's opening address honored men and women of peace whose efforts led to the founding of the United Nations. He noted Eleanor Roosevelt in particular:

> *Among them there is one delegate to whom I wish to extend particular sympathy and tribute. ... I do not think it would be possible to begin this Assembly without mentioning her and the name of the late President Roosevelt and expressing our conviction that his disappearance was a great grief to us all and an irreparable loss.*

Because so many of the positions Roosevelt supported were controversial at the time, the FBI compiled a large file of materials concerning her views and activities. Her support of the United Nations particularly threatened FBI Director J. Edgar Hoover, who believed it meant she was connected with communists. As a result, Roosevelt's FBI file is one of the largest in American history.

Among the early concerns of the United Nations were human rights. Roosevelt headed the Human Rights Commission and helped draft its Declaration of Human Rights. She asked people to consider,

"When will our consciences grow so tender that we will act to prevent human misery rather than avenge it?" Roosevelt's goal was to set up what she called a "Magna Carta for mankind"—a list of rights to which every human being is entitled.

In 1948, Roosevelt spoke in Paris about the struggle for human rights. She said:

> *We must not be confused about what freedom is. Basic human rights are simple and easily understood: freedom of speech and a free press, freedom of religion and worship; freedom of assembly and the right of petition; the right of men to be secure in their homes and free from unreasonable search and seizure and from arbitrary arrest and punishment.*
>
> *Freedom for our people is not only a right, but also a tool. Freedom of speech, freedom of the press, freedom of information, freedom of assembly—they are not just abstract ideals to us; they are tools with which we create a way of life, a way of life in which we can enjoy freedom.*

The Declaration of Human Rights passed unanimously in the U.N. General Assembly.

In the United States, President Harry Truman announced in 1952 that he would not seek another term as president. General Dwight D. Eisenhower ran as a Republican against Democrat Adlai

Stevenson. Eisenhower won, and he immediately asked for Roosevelt's resignation from the United Nations. She said:

The Declaration of Human Rights, shown in Spanish, was approved by all U.N. voting countries.

> *The General lost no time in firing me. It was one of his first acts after being elected. I told him that as all ambassadors automatically resign when a new president is elected, my resignation would have been on his desk by December 31, but he couldn't wait.*

85

Roosevelt resigned from her U.N. position when General Dwight D. Eisenhower became president.

So, Roosevelt went home. She read to her grandchildren in the evenings and continued to write "My Day." But she never gave up promoting the United Nations. She wasn't a delegate, but she supported the activities the best she could. At one point, Roosevelt's agent asked if she would consider doing a margarine commercial for TV. The work paid $35,000. The agent pointed out that doing the commercial would open her up to criticism, but that wasn't news to Roosevelt. She decided the criticism was worth it. The $35,000 she'd earn would buy

6,000 CARE packages, sent from the United Nations to needy people around the world.

Her agent was right. The letters poured in, half good and half bad. "The mail was evenly divided," she said. "One half was sad because I had damaged my reputation. The other half was happy because I had damaged my reputation."

Roosevelt enjoyed being a mother and a grandmother. She visited her children as often as possible. In a 1954 "My Day" column, she remarked on a new game she and her grandchildren played:

> *I was introduced to Scrabble, which practically has become an obsession with some of us. Those who play it know how competitive one can become in finding combinations of words. ... I am so bad at games ... that I always find I can start and teach the children and then they rapidly become so much more proficient that I am again relegated to my knitting.*

In 1957, Roosevelt went to the Soviet Union to write a series of articles and to interview Premier Nikita Khrushchev. When she arrived in the country, she had to have all her travel plans approved by the government. In communist Russia, she was not free to go wherever she wanted, and neither could ordinary citizens. Roosevelt toured farms, hospitals, and schools, both in Moscow and outside the capital.

For her interview with Premier Khrushchev, Roosevelt provided Khrushchev with a list of questions before their meeting. For days, she heard nothing about her plans for the interview. Then, one day her Russian interpreter told her to be ready to go to a meeting with Khrushchev. Roosevelt and Khrushchev did not agree about many things. The size of and need for a large army was one of them. At the end of their meeting, Roosevelt asked him if she could say their conversation had been friendly. Krushchev smiled and answered, "At least we didn't shoot at each other."

Roosevelt interviewed Soviet Premier Nikita Khrushchev with the aid of an interpreter.

Two years later, Khrushchev came to the United States. The State Department decided that he should visit Eleanor at the Franklin D. Roosevelt Library in Hyde Park. The Secret Service looked the library over and determined that the only way to keep Khrushchev safe was to have him come in and leave by the rear exit. The Soviet Embassy said that would be an insult. Forever the diplomat, Eleanor Roosevelt came up with a solution. They would hang signs by the rear entrance that said, "Main Entrance." The visit went off without a hitch.

Another famous visitor that year made a lasting impression on Roosevelt. In 1959, Mohammed Riza Pahlavi was shah of Iran, a ruler wealthy beyond imagination. When he visited Roosevelt at Hyde Park, the two toured her late husband's library. The shah showed Roosevelt a rug he had given to her husband. He explained the tremendous number of knots required to make the rug, saying that only the tiny hands of the youngest children were capable of tying them. Roosevelt winced. She had battled against child labor and having such a rug, made by the hands of children, on the Roosevelt library floor upset her deeply. ❧

9 MILESTONES

Chapter

❧◉❧

As Dwight D. Eisenhower's eight years as president came to a close, two Democrats were vying to take over his job: Lyndon Johnson and John F. Kennedy. Now in her 70s, Roosevelt still had the respect of the Democratic Party. Both men wanted her support.

Roosevelt said of Johnson, "He wants to be president, but … I couldn't learn about a single program he had formulated." She pointed out that the only reason her husband had wanted to be president was because it gave him the power to make changes, not because he wanted power for its own sake. Johnson, she feared, was power hungry without a purpose.

John F. Kennedy also called on Roosevelt. Again, she hesitated to support him. When asked why, she explained that he had not shown her the "strong

Roosevelt supported John F. Kennedy as a presidential candidate and spoke at the "Citizens for Kennedy" headquarters in 1960.

convictions and the courage to act on them [that] were the prerequisites for command leadership." She promised she would support his candidacy if Kennedy demonstrated his support of the basic values of Democrats and showed that he could and would lead the Democratic Party. Kennedy followed her advice, and Roosevelt supported him for president.

It was not surprising that, after the election, President Kennedy asked Eleanor Roosevelt to be on his Commission on the Status of Women. It was her last major opportunity to work for the equality of women in society.

At that point, Roosevelt was already dying. She had been diagnosed with a rare bone marrow disease in 1960. She had about two years to live after the diagnosis and, as was typical of her, she meant to make every day worth something. She wrote:

> *I could not, at any age, be content to take my place in a corner by the fireside and simply look on. Life was meant to be lived. ... One must never, for whatever reason, turn his back on life.*

Efficient to the end, Roosevelt planned her funeral well in advance. She wanted a plain oak casket covered in pine boughs from the Roosevelt family's Hyde Park estate. She didn't want flowers—and her wish was fulfilled.

Eleanor Roosevelt died on November 7, 1962. She was 78. Among the politicians attending her funeral were President John F. Kennedy and first lady Jacqueline Kennedy, former President and Mrs. Eisenhower, Vice President and Mrs. Johnson, and former President and Mrs. Truman. Representatives from nations around the world honored Roosevelt by attending the funeral. Marian Anderson, the African-American singer who owed so much to Roosevelt, was also there to pay her last respects.

Three former presidents and one president attended Eleanor Roosevelt's funeral.

At the funeral service, politician and diplomat Adlai Stevenson said:

> *What other single human being has touched and transformed the existence of so many? ... She walked in the slums ... of the world, not on a tour of inspection ... but as one who could not feel contentment when others were hungry.*

In her honor, President Kennedy ordered that flags on public buildings be flown at half-staff. This was the first time a former first lady was honored in this way.

Eleanor Roosevelt was many things: activist, reformer, mother, wife, diplomat—the list goes on and on. She mixed her talents for writing and speaking with her desire to build a better world. And she succeeded. Kind, gentle, and interested, she made every person she spoke to feel important.

Eleanor Roosevelt often said that Franklin might have preferred a different wife—one who was completely uncritical of his actions. Had that been so, the nation would have lost its greatest first lady. To the end, she

After her death, Roosevelt's son Elliott wrote a series of best-selling fictional murder mysteries in which first lady Eleanor Roosevelt acts as a detective, helping the police solve crimes. They feature actual places and celebrities of the time.

believed in people's ability to be good to one another and find a lasting peace. "This I believe with all my heart," she said. "If we want a free and peaceful world, if we want to make the desert bloom and man grow to greater dignity as a human being— we can do it!" 🍂

In 1963, the U.S. Postal Service issued a stamp in honor of the late Eleanor Roosevelt.

ROOSEVELT'S LIFE

1905
Marries Franklin
Delano Roosevelt

1884
Born in
New York City

1899–1902
Attends Allenswood
School, near
London, England

1900

1903
Brothers Orville and
Wilbur Wright
successfully fly a
powered airplane

1893
Women gain voting
privileges in New
Zealand, the first
country to take such
a step

WORLD EVENTS

1918

Works with the Red Cross and Navy to help servicemen in World War I

1920

Becomes a member of the League of Women Voters

1920

1916

German-born physicist Albert Einstein publishes his general theory of relativity

1919

World War I peace conference begins at Versailles, France

ROOSEVELT'S LIFE

1936
Begins writing "My Day" column

1933
Becomes first lady when husband is inaugurated as president

1930

1933
Nazi leader Adolf Hitler is named chancellor of Germany

1939
German troops invade Poland; Britain and France declare war on Germany; World War II (1939–1945) begins

WORLD EVENTS

1943

Travels to the South
Pacific to visit
American servicemen

1945

Franklin dies; World
War II ends; serves as
a delegate to the new
United Nations

1945

1945

The United Nations
is founded

ROOSEVELT'S LIFE

1957
Visits the
Soviet Union

1947
Becomes chairperson
of the U.N. Human
Rights Commission

1950

1949
The People's Republic
of China is
established

1953
The first Europeans
climb Mount Everest

WORLD EVENTS

1962

Dies on November 7

1961

Appointed as chairperson of the President's Commission on the Status of Women

1960

1961

Soviet cosmonaut Yuri Gagarin is the first human to enter space

1962

Pope John XXIII calls the Second Vatican Council, modernizing Roman Catholicism

NAME: Anna Eleanor Roosevelt

DATE OF BIRTH: October 11, 1884

BIRTHPLACE: New York City, New York

FATHER: Elliott Roosevelt

MOTHER: Anna Hall Roosevelt

EDUCATION: Allenswood School, England

SPOUSE: Franklin Delano Roosevelt (1882–1945)

DATE OF MARRIAGE: March 17, 1905

CHILDREN: Anna (1906–1975)

James (1907–1991)

Franklin Junior (1909)

Elliott (1910–1990)

Franklin Junior (1914–1988)

John (1916–1981)

DATE OF DEATH: November 7, 1962

PLACE OF BURIAL: Hyde Park, New York

IN THE LIBRARY

Cooper, Michael L. *Dust to East: Drought and Depression in the 1930s.* New York: Clarion Books, 2004.

Freedman, Russell. *Eleanor Roosevelt: A Life of Discovery.* Boston: Houghton, Mifflin, 1997.

Gottfried, Ted. *Eleanor Roosevelt: First Lady of the 20th Century.* New York: Franklin Watts, 1997.

Stein, R. Conrad. *The World War II D-Day Invasion in American History.* Berkeley Heights, N.J.: Enslow Publishers, 2004.

Thompson, Gare. *Who Was Eleanor Roosevelt?* New York: Grosset & Dunlap, 2004.

Waxman, Laura Hamilton. *Franklin D. Roosevelt.* Minneapolis: Lerner Publications, 2004.

LOOK FOR MORE SIGNATURE LIVES
BOOKS ABOUT THIS ERA:

Andrew Carnegie: *Captain of Industry*

Carrie Chapman Catt: *A Voice for Women*

Henry B. Gonzalez: *Congressman of the People*

J. Edgar Hoover: *Controversial FBI Director*

Langston Hughes: *The Voice of Harlem*

Douglas MacArthur: *America's General*

Elizabeth Cady Stanton: *Social Reformer*

ON THE WEB

For more information on *Eleanor Roosevelt,* use FactHound to track down Web sites related to this book.

1. Go to *www.facthound.com*
2. Type in a search word related to this book or this book ID: 0756509920
3. Click on the *Fetch It* button.

FactHound will find the best Web sites for you.

HISTORIC SITES

Eleanor Roosevelt National Historic Site
4097 Albany Post Road
Hyde Park, NY 12538
845/229-9115
To see Eleanor Roosevelt's home, the only National Historic Site dedicated to a first lady

Eleanor Roosevelt Gallery
Franklin D. Roosevelt Presidential Libary and Museum
4097 Albany Post Road
Hyde Park, NY 12538
800/337-8474
To see a biographical exhibit featuring items from Roosevelt's life

alcoholic
a person who suffers from a disease in which he or she has a strong, uncontrollable desire to drink beer, wine, or liquor

canteen
a meeting place sponsored by a church or other civic group

communist
one who supports an economic system in which property is owned by the government or community and profits are shared

debutante
a young woman who is making her debut in society

discrimination
the act of treating a person as inferior because of his or her sex, race, or religion

investments
money lent to something, such as a company, in the belief that one will get more money back in the future

malnutrition
the state in which a human body does not take in sufficient food to maintain good health

rationing
a program that limited people from buying certain goods, usually to prevent overbuying and hoarding

segregation
the act of keeping races separate by law or deed

suffrage movement
the political actions taken to get women the right to vote

sweatshop
an inferior workplace where people work long hours for little pay in horrible working conditions

Chapter 1

Page 10, line 1: Eleanor Roosevelt. Letter to the DAR. 26 February 1939.
http://www.fdrlibrary.marist.edu/tmirhfee.html

Chapter 2

Page 14, line 8: Eleanor Roosevelt. *The Autobiography of Eleanor Roosevelt.*
New York: Da Capo Press, 1992, p. 5.

Page 14, line 22: Ibid., p. 6.

Page 14, line 25: Joseph P. Lash. *Eleanor and Franklin.* New York:
W. W. Norton & Company, 1971, p. 30.

Page 17, line 5: *The Autobiography of Eleanor Roosevelt,* p. 7.

Page 18, line 7: *Eleanor and Franklin,* p. 45.

Chapter 3

Page 27, line 7: *Eleanor and Franklin,* p. 100.

Page 29, line 25: Ibid., p. 147.

Page 32, line 23: Joseph P. Lash. *Life Was Meant to Be Lived.* New York:
W. W. Norton & Company, 1984, p. 20.

Chapter 4

Page 35, line 10: *Life Was Meant to Be Lived,* p. 20.

Page 37, line 19: *The Autobiography of Eleanor Roosevelt,* p. 75.

Page 38, line 16: *Life Was Meant to Be Lived,* p. 30.

Page 41, line 10: Joseph P. Lash. *Love, Eleanor.* Garden City, N.Y.: Doubleday,
1982, p. 66.

Chapter 5

Page 50, line 2: *Life Was Meant to Be Lived,* p. 57.

Page 52, line 21: Eleanor Roosevelt. *My Day.* David Emblidge, ed. New York:
Da Capo Press, 2001, p. 25.

Page 54, line 2: Ibid., p. 12.

Page 55, line 7: Robin Gerber. *Leadership the Eleanor Roosevelt Way.*
New York: Penguin Books, 2002, p. 166.

Page 55, line 1: *My Day,* p. 186.

Page 57, line 19: Blanche Wiesen Cook. *Eleanor Roosevelt: Volume 2:
1933–1938.* New York: Penguin Books, 1999, p. 71.

Chapter 6

Page 60, line 1: Eleanor Roosevelt. "How to Take Criticism." *Ladies' Home
Journal.* November 1944.

Page 61, line 12: *My Day,* p. 8.

Page 62, line 25: *Leadership the Eleanor Roosevelt Way,* p. 180.

Page 64, line 1: "Tuskegee Airmen: History"
http://www.acepilots.com/usaaf_tusk.html.

Page 65, line 3: Franklin D. Roosevelt. Address to Congress. 8 December 1941.

Chapter 7

Page 68, line 1: *The Autobiography of Eleanor Roosevelt*, p. 251.

Page 68, line 26: Eleanor Roosevelt. Letter to Cecil Peterson. 16 July 1942. http://www.fedlibrary/marist.edu/tusktxt.html

Page 71, line 15: *My Day*, p. 72.

Page 72, sidebar: "Eleanor Roosevelt's Wartime Prayer." The Eleanor Roosevelt Papers. http://www.gwu.edu/~erpapers/abouteleanor/q-and-a/q21-prayer.htm

Page 72, line 18: *Eleanor and Franklin*, p. 662.

Page 73, line 5: Ibid., p. 668.

Page 74, line 14: *The Autobiography of Eleanor Roosevelt*, p. 255.

Page 75, line 7: William F. Halsey and J. Bryan. *Admiral Halsey's Story*. New York: Whittlesey House, 1947, p. 167.

Page 77, line 2: *Leadership the Eleanor Roosevelt Way*, p. 205.

Page 77, line 10: *The Autobiography of Eleanor Roosevelt*, p. 276.

Page 78, line 4: *Leadership the Eleanor Roosevelt Way*, p. 206.

Page 79, line 13: *The Autobiography of Eleanor Roosevelt*, p. 280.

Chapter 8

Page 82, line 5: Joseph P. Lash. *Eleanor: The Years Alone*. New York: W. W. Norton & Sons, 1972, p. 38.

Page 83, line 15: Ibid., p. 45.

Page 84, line 1: *Life Was Meant to Be Lived*, p. 147.

Page 84, line 8: Eleanor Roosevelt. "The Struggle for Human Rights." http://www.gwu.edu/erpapers/documents/speeches/doc026617.html

Page 85, line 4: William Turner Levy and Cynthia Eagle Russett. *The Extraordinary Mrs. R.* New York: John Wiley & Sons, 1999, p. 92.

Page 87, line 4: *Eleanor: The Years Alone*, p. 304.

Page 87, line 12: *My Day*, p. 213.

Page 88, line 11: *The Autobiography of Eleanor Roosevelt*, p. 383.

Chapter 9

Page 91, line 6: *The Extraordinary Mrs. R.*, p. 205.

Page 91, line 15: Ibid., p. 210.

Page 92, line 19: *Eleanor: The Years Alone*, p. 303.

Page 94, line 3: William Chafe. "Biographical Essay." The Papers of Eleanor Roosevelt. http://www.lexisnexis.com/academic/guides/womens_studies/eroos.asp.

Page 95, line 2: *Eleanor: The Years Alone*, p. 327.

Chafe, William. "Biographical Essay." The Papers of Eleanor Roosevelt. http://www.lexisnexis.com/academic/guides/womens_studies/eroos.asp.

Cook, Blanche Wiesen. *Eleanor Roosevelt: Volume 1: 1884–1933.* New York: Penguin Books, 1992.

Cook, Blanche Wiesen. *Eleanor Roosevelt: Volume 2: 1933–1938.* New York: Penguin Books, 1999.

Gerber, Robin. *Leadership the Eleanor Roosevelt Way.* New York: Penguin Books, 2002.

Halsey, William F., and J. Bryan. *Admiral Halsey's Story.* New York: Whittlesey House, 1947.

Lash, Joseph P. *Eleanor and Franklin.* New York: W. W. Norton & Company, 1971.

Lash, Joseph P. *Eleanor: The Years Alone.* New York: W. W. Norton & Sons, 1972.

Lash, Joseph P. *Life Was Meant to Be Lived.* New York: W. W. Norton & Company, 1984.

Levy, William Turner, and Cynthia Eagle Russett. *The Extraordinary Mrs. R.* New York: John Wiley & Sons, 1999.

Roosevelt, Eleanor. "Are We Overlooking the Pursuit of Happiness?" *Parents.* September 1936.

Roosevelt, Eleanor. *The Autobiography of Eleanor Roosevelt.* New York: Da Capo Press, 1992.

Roosevelt, Eleanor. "Building Character." *Parents.* June 1931,

Roosevelt, Eleanor. "How to Take Criticism." *Ladies' Home Journal.* November 1944.

Barbara A. Somervill has been writing for more than 30 years. She has written newspaper and magazine articles, video scripts, and books for children. She enjoys writing about science and investigating people's lives for biographies. Ms. Somervill lives with her husband in South Carolina.

Image Credits

Bettmann/Corbis, cover (all), 2, 4-5, 51, 60, 73, 75, 78, 86, 88, 98 (top), 99 (top left), 100 (top right); Library of Congress, 8, 26, 29, 45, 49, 58, 63, 69, 90, 95, 97, 98 (bottom, all); Hulton Archive/Getty Images, 11, 101 (top); Franklin D. Roosevelt Library, 12, 15, 16, 19, 21, 23, 24, 30, 33, 36, 39, 46, 53, 56, 66, 85, 96 (top, all), 100 (top left); Corbis, 34, 54, 93; DVIC/NARA, 40; Time Life Pictures/U.S. Navy/Getty Images, 65; Harold M. Lambert/Lambert/Getty Images, 70; Hulton-Deutsch Collection/Corbis, 77; Keystone/Getty Images, 80, 99 (top right); NASA, 96 (bottom), 101 (bottom); Corel, 99 (bottom), 100 (bottom right); Brand X Pictures, 100 (bottom left).